Today's English Version

AMERICAN BIBLE SOCIETY
NEW YORK

This is a Portion of Holy Scripture in *Today's English Version* from the *Good News Bible*. The American Bible Society is a not-for-profit organization which publishes Scriptures without doctrinal note or comment. Since 1816, its single mission has been to make the Word of God easily available to people everywhere at the lowest possible cost and in the languages they understand best. Working toward this goal, the ABS is a member of the United Bible Societies, a worldwide effort that extends to more than 180 countries and territories. You are urged to read the Bible and to share it with others. For a free catalog of other Scripture publications, call the American Bible Society at 1-800-32-BIBLE, or write to 1865 Broadway, New York, NY 10023-7505. Visit the ABS website! www.americanbible.org.

Copyright © 1992, American Bible Society

Printed in the United States of America
Eng. Port. TEV560 – 104720
ABS – 1/00 – 2,000 – 20,900 – LC9

GOD'S LOVE NEVER FAILS

God's unfailing love is demonstrated in many ways. Several biblical writers describe how they have experienced God's love, but only in Jesus Christ is that love fully revealed.

God's Love Never Fails focuses upon the *nature* and *demands* of divine love as reflected in the writings of Moses, David, Hosea, Paul, James, Peter and John. The final section contains passages from the Gospel of John, which emphasize what Jesus taught and did to reveal God's love.

The word *demands* is used when speaking of God's love because God's love always invites a response. As you read what these biblical writers have to say about God's love, take time to read and reflect on the questions at the end of each chapter. Ask yourself what response you are able to make to God's gracious expression of love for you!

CONTENTS

Ask Moses about God's Love	1
Ask David about God's Love	7
Ask Hosea about God's Love	15
Ask Paul about God's Love	19
Ask James, Peter and John about God's Love	25
Ask Jesus about God's Love	31

ASK MOSES ABOUT GOD'S LOVE

During the time of Israel's wanderings through the desert, Moses spoke to the people on several occasions about the never failing character of God's love.

You must love God with all your heart

"Israel, remember this! The LORD—and the LORD alone—is our God. Love the LORD your God with all your heart, with all your soul, and with all your strength. Never forget these commands that I am giving you today. Teach them to your children. Repeat them when you are at home and when you are away, when you are resting and when you are working. Tie them on your arms and wear them on your foreheads as a reminder. Write them on the doorposts of your houses and on your gates."

Deutoronomy 6.4-9

2

God's love demands love and obedience

"Now, people of Israel, listen to what the LORD your God demands of you: Worship the LORD and do all that he commands. Love him, serve him with all your heart, and obey all his laws. I am giving them to you today for your benefit. To the LORD belong even the highest heavens; the earth is his also, and everything on it. But the LORD's love for your ancestors was so strong that he chose you instead of any other people, and you are still his chosen people. So then, from now on be obedient to the LORD and stop being stubborn. The LORD your God is supreme over all gods and over all powers. He is great and mighty, and he is to be obeyed. He does not show partiality, and he does not accept bribes. He makes sure that orphans and widows are treated fairly; he loves the foreigners who live with our people, and gives them food and clothes. So then, show love for those foreigners, because you were once foreigners in Egypt. Have reverence for the LORD your God and worship only him. Be faithful to him and make your promises in his name alone. Praise him—he is your God, and you have seen with your own eyes the great and astounding things that he has done for you. When your ancestors went to Egypt, there were only seventy of them. But now the LORD your God has made you as numerous as the stars in the sky."

Deuteronomy 10.12-22

3

God shows his love to those who love him

"The LORD did not love you and choose you because you outnumbered other peoples; you were the smallest nation on earth. But the LORD loved you and wanted to keep the promise that he made to your ancestors. That is why he saved you by his great might and set you free from slavery to the king of Egypt. Remember that the LORD your God is the only God and that he is faithful. He will keep his covenant and show his constant love to a thousand generations of those who love him and obey his commands, but he will not hesitate to punish those who hate him. Now then, obey what you have been taught; obey all the laws that I have given you today."

Deuteronomy 7.7-11

"Today I am giving you a choice between good and evil, between life and death. If you obey the commands of the LORD your God, which I give you today, if you love him, obey him, and keep all his laws, then you will prosper and become a nation of many people. The LORD your God will bless you in the land that you are about to occupy. But if you disobey and refuse to listen, and are led away to worship other gods, you will be destroyed—I warn you here and now. You will not live long in that land across the Jordan that you are about to occupy. I am now giving you the choice between life and death, between God's blessing and God's curse, and I call heaven and earth to witness the choice you make. Choose life.

4

Love the LORD your God, obey him and be faithful to him, and then you and your descendants will live long in the land that he promised to give your ancestors, Abraham, Isaac, and Jacob."

Deuteronomy 30.15-20

Review and reflect

1. List the kinds of things you think of when you hear the word "love." Circle every occurrence of the word "love" in this chapter. Re-read the sentences they occur in. Add to your list any additional descriptions of the word "love."

2. Moses tells the people of Israel to "Love the LORD your God with all your heart, with all your soul, and with all your strength." Make a list of the ways you can show your love for God with all your heart, soul, and strength.

3. Underline or highlight the phrases in this chapter that describe God's love. Write in the margins some adjectives that summarize these thoughts. Do people today show love for one another in the same way? Why or why not?

4. Moses reminds the people of Israel that God loved them so much that he freed them from a life of slavery. Are there areas in your life where you feel enslaved? If so, what are they?

5. Moses challenges the people of Israel to choose "between good and evil, between life and death." What do you think Moses meant when he told them to "choose life"? If you were challenged to do that today, how do you think you would respond?

ASK DAVID ABOUT GOD'S LOVE

David sings of God's constant love

O LORD, I will always sing of your
  constant love;
 I will proclaim your faithfulness forever.
I know that your love will last for all time,
 that your faithfulness is as permanent
  as the sky.
You said, "I have made a covenant with
  the man I chose;
 I have promised my servant David,
'A descendant of yours will always be king;
 I will preserve your dynasty forever.' "

The heavens sing of the wonderful things
  you do;
 the holy ones sing of your faithfulness,
  LORD.
No one in heaven is like you, LORD;
 none of the heavenly beings is your equal.
You are feared in the council of the
  holy ones;
 they all stand in awe of you.

Lord God Almighty, none is as mighty
   as you;
  in all things you are faithful, O Lord.
You rule over the powerful sea;
  you calm its angry waves.
You crushed the monster Rahab and
   killed it;
  with your mighty strength you
   defeated your enemies.
Heaven is yours, the earth also;
  you made the world and everything in it.
You created the north and the south;
  Mount Tabor and Mount Hermon sing
   to you for joy.
How powerful you are!
  How great is your strength!
Your kingdom is founded on righteousness
   and justice;
  love and faithfulness are shown in all
   you do.

How happy are the people who worship
   you with songs,
  who live in the light of your kindness!
Because of you they rejoice all day long,
  and they praise you for your goodness.
You give us great victories;
  in your love you make us triumphant.
You, O Lord, chose our protector;
  you, the Holy God of Israel, gave us our
   king.

Psalm 89.1-18

David can worship because of God's great love

Listen to my words, O LORD,
  and hear my sighs.
Listen to my cry for help,
  my God and king!

I pray to you, O LORD;
  you hear my voice in the morning;
at sunrise I offer my prayer
  and wait for your answer.

You are not a God who is pleased with wrongdoing;
  you allow no evil in your presence.
You cannot stand the sight of the proud;
  you hate all wicked people.
You destroy all liars
  and despise violent, deceitful people.

But because of your great love
  I can come into your house;
I can worship in your holy Temple
  and bow down to you in reverence.
LORD, I have so many enemies!
  Lead me to do your will;
  make your way plain for me to follow.

What my enemies say can never be trusted;
  they only want to destroy.
Their words are flattering and smooth,
  but full of deadly deceit.

Condemn and punish them, O God;
  may their own plots cause their ruin.
Drive them out of your presence
  because of their many sins
  and their rebellion against you.

But all who find safety in you will rejoice;
  they can always sing for joy.
Protect those who love you;
  because of you they are truly happy.
You bless those who obey you, LORD;
  your love protects them like a shield.

Psalm 5

David relies on God's constant love

How much longer will you forget me, LORD?
  Forever?
How much longer will you hide yourself
  from me?
How long must I endure trouble?
  How long will sorrow fill my heart day
  and night?
  How long will my enemies triumph
  over me?

Look at me, O LORD my God, and
  answer me.
  Restore my strength; don't let me die.
Don't let my enemies say, "We have
  defeated him."
  Don't let them gloat over my downfall.

I rely on your constant love;
  I will be glad, because you will rescue me.
I will sing to you, O LORD,
  because you have been good to me.

Psalm 13

God's constant love protects his people

LORD, your constant love reaches the heavens;
  your faithfulness extends to the skies.
Your righteousness is towering like the mountains;
  your justice is like the depths of the sea.
People and animals are in your care.

How precious, O God, is your constant love!
  We find protection under the shadow of your wings.
We feast on the abundant food you provide;
  you let us drink from the river of your goodness.
You are the source of all life,
  and because of your light we see the light.

Psalm 36. 5-9

Those who know God's love and loyalty love to do his will

You do not want sacrifices and offerings;
  you do not ask for animals burned whole on the altar
  or for sacrifices to take away sins.

Instead, you have given me ears to
   hear you,
  and so I answered, "Here I am;
  your instructions for me are in the book
   of the Law.
How I love to do your will, my God!
  I keep your teaching in my heart."

In the assembly of all your people, LORD,
  I told the good news that you save us.
  You know that I will never stop telling it.
I have not kept the news of salvation to
   myself;
  I have always spoken of your faithfulness
   and help.

In the assembly of all your people I have
   not been silent
  about your loyalty and constant love.

LORD, I know you will never stop being
   merciful to me.
  Your love and loyalty will always keep
   me safe.

Psalm 40.6-11

Review and reflect

1. In Psalm 89, David sings of God's constant love. What things does he sing about? Underline or highlight them in your book.

2. Many of the Psalms of the Bible were originally written as songs of worship. Write song lyrics about God's love for you. (Don't worry about making it rhyme or setting it to music.) What things did you mention in your song? What did you learn about your relationship with God from this exercise?

3. In Psalm 13, David says, "How much longer will you forget me, LORD? Forever? How much longer will you hide yourself from me?" Why do you think David said this? What do you think he was feeling? Have you ever felt this way? If so, when? What did you do?

4. Several of the Psalms in this chapter focus on the protection God provides. Circle all the occurrences of words that relate to the theme of protection (such as, "protector," "safety," and "shield"). When in your life do you feel safest? When don't you feel safe at all? Write another song, this time about the protection God offers you. Use this song in your prayers the next time you feel scared or uncertain.

ASK HOSEA ABOUT GOD'S LOVE

The prophet Hosea compared God's love for Israel to that of a loyal husband whose love for his wife was unfailing, even when she was unfaithful to him.

God's love includes those who are unloved and unlovely

Israel, I will make you my wife;
 I will be true and faithful;
 I will show you constant love and mercy
 and make you mine forever.
I will keep my promise and make you mine,
 and you will acknowledge me as LORD.
At that time I will answer the prayers of my people Israel.
 I will make rain fall on the earth,
 and the earth will produce grain and grapes and olives.
I will establish my people in the land
 and make them prosper.

I will show love to those who were called
"Unloved,"
and to those who were called
"Not-My-People"
I will say, "You are my people,"
and they will answer, "You are our God."

Hosea 2.19-23

Through love God draws his unfaithful people back

The LORD says,
"When Israel was a child, I loved him
and called him out of Egypt as my son.
But the more I called to him,
the more he turned away from me.
My people sacrificed to Baal;
they burned incense to idols.
Yet I was the one who taught Israel
to walk.
I took my people up in my arms,
but they did not acknowledge that I
took care of them.
I drew them to me with affection and love.
I picked them up and held them to
my cheek;
I bent down to them and fed them."

Hosea 11.1-4

God's love will not let him destroy his people

"How can I give you up, Israel?
How can I abandon you?

Could I ever destroy you as I did Admah,
  or treat you as I did Zeboiim?
My heart will not let me do it!
  My love for you is too strong.
I will not punish you in my anger;
  I will not destroy Israel again.
For I am God and not a mere human being.
  I, the Holy One, am with you.
I will not come to you in anger."

Hosea 11.8,9

God's love is his people's hope

The LORD says,
  "I will bring my people back to me.
I will love them with all my heart;
  no longer am I angry with them.
I will be to the people of Israel
  like rain in a dry land.
They will blossom like flowers;
  they will be firmly rooted
  like the trees of Lebanon.
They will be alive with new growth,
  and beautiful like olive trees.
They will be fragrant
  like the cedars of Lebanon.
Once again they will live under my
    protection.
They will grow crops of grain
  and be fruitful like a vineyard.
  They will be as famous as the wine of
    Lebanon.
The people of Israel will have nothing more
    to do with idols;

> I will answer their prayers and take care of them.
> Like an evergreen tree I will shelter them;
> I am the source of all their blessings."
>
> *Hosea 14.4-8*

Review and reflect

1. In the first passage of this chapter, Hosea compares God's love for Israel to that of a loyal husband for his wife. Underline or highlight the words in this section that describe the kind of husband God is.

2. In the second passage, Hosea compares God's love for Israel to that of a caring parent. Underline or highlight those words that describe the things that God did for Israel.

3. Think about these two images (loyal husband, caring parent) and look at the words you have underlined. Do you feel God cares for you in the same way? Why or why not?

4. In the last passage of this chapter, two more images of God's love are given. What are they? Are they good descriptions for God's love? Why or why not?

5. Have you ever had an opportunity to offer someone protection? Why did you do it? How did it make you feel? How did it affect your relationship with that person?

ASK PAUL ABOUT GOD'S LOVE

God's love sets us free to serve one another

As for you, my friends, you were called to be free. But do not let this freedom become an excuse for letting your physical desires control you. Instead, let love make you serve one another. For the whole Law is summed up in one commandment: "Love your neighbor as you love yourself." But if you act like wild animals, hurting and harming each other, then watch out, or you will completely destroy one another.

Galatians 5.13-15

Love must be completely sincere

Love must be completely sincere. Hate what is evil, hold on to what is good. Love one another warmly as Christians, and be eager to show respect for one another. Work hard and do not be lazy. Serve the Lord with a heart full of devotion. Let your hope keep you joyful, be patient in your troubles, and pray at all times. Share your belongings with your needy fellow Christians, and open your homes to strangers.

Ask God to bless those who persecute you—yes, ask him to bless, not to curse. Be happy with those who are happy, weep with those who weep. Have the same concern for everyone. Do not be proud, but accept humble duties. Do not think of yourselves as wise.

If someone has done you wrong, do not repay him with a wrong. Try to do what everyone considers to be good. Do everything possible on your part to live in peace with everybody. Never take revenge, my friends, but instead let God's anger do it. For the scripture says, "I will take revenge, I will pay back, says the Lord." Instead, as the scripture says: "If your enemies are hungry, feed them; if they are thirsty, give them a drink; for by doing this you will make them burn with shame." Do not let evil defeat you; instead, conquer evil with good.

Romans 12.9-21

The Christian's only obligation is to love

Be under obligation to no one—the only obligation you have is to love one another. Whoever does this has obeyed the Law. The commandments, "Do not commit adultery; do not commit murder; do not steal; do not desire what belongs to someone else"—all these, and any others besides, are summed up in the one command, "Love your neighbor as you love yourself." If you love others, you will never do them wrong; to love, then, is to obey the whole Law.

You must do this, because you know that the time has come for you to wake up from your sleep. For the moment when we will be saved is closer now than it was when we first believed. The night is nearly over, day is almost here. Let us stop doing the things that belong to the dark, and let us take up weapons for fighting in the light. Let us conduct ourselves properly, as people who live in the light of day—no orgies or drunkenness, no immorality or indecency, no fighting or jealousy.

Romans 13.8-13

Love is greater than anything else

I may be able to speak the languages of human beings and even of angels, but if I have no love, my speech is no more than a noisy gong or a clanging bell. I may have the gift of inspired preaching; I may have all knowledge and understand all secrets; I may have all the faith needed to move mountains—but if I have no love, I am nothing. I may give away everything I have, and even give up my body to be burned—but if I have no love, this does me no good.

Love is patient and kind; it is not jealous or conceited or proud; love is not ill-mannered or selfish or irritable; love does not keep a record of wrongs; love is not happy with evil, but is happy with the truth. Love never gives up; and its faith, hope, and patience never fail.

Love is eternal. There are inspired messages, but they are temporary; there are gifts of speaking in strange tongues, but they will cease; there is knowledge, but it will pass. For our gifts of knowledge and of inspired messages are only partial; but when what is perfect comes, then what is partial will disappear.

When I was a child, my speech, feelings, and thinking were all those of a child; now that I am an adult, I have no more use for childish ways. What we see now is like a dim image in a mirror; then we shall see face-to-face. What I know now is only partial; then it will be complete—as complete as God's knowledge of me.

Meanwhile these three remain: faith, hope, and love; and the greatest of these is love.

1 Corinthians 13

Review and reflect

*1. What do you think is meant by "Love your neighbor as you love yourself?" What is meant by "your neighbor"? List the ways you can show love toward your neighbor. Compare this list with the one you did at the beginning for question #3 in the section, **Ask Moses about God's Love**. How are these lists the same? How are they different?*

2. Love is more than a nice feeling. In the section "Love must be completely sincere," Paul describes love in action. Highlight and list all the "action phrases" that describe something love enables you to do. When has your love led you to serve others? How did that make you feel?

23

3. In the section "The Christian's only obligation is to love," Paul says, "If you love others, you will never do them wrong." When has your love for someone kept you from doing something harmful? Make a list of behaviors that you would consider "unloving" or harmful.

4. How does Paul describe love in the last section of this chapter? Highlight words and phrases that describe love. Now try this exercise. Re-read the sentences where you have highlighted words but replace "love" with "God." Now re-read the passage again replacing the phrase "love is" or "love does" with "I am" or "I do." What feelings or thoughts came to mind as you did this exercise?

ASK JAMES, PETER AND JOHN ABOUT GOD'S LOVE

Love shows no favoritism

My friends, as believers in our Lord Jesus Christ, the Lord of glory, you must never treat people in different ways according to their outward appearance. Suppose a rich man wearing a gold ring and fine clothes comes to your meeting, and a poor man in ragged clothes also comes. If you show more respect to the well-dressed man and say to him, "Have this best seat here," but say to the poor man, "Stand over there, or sit here on the floor by my feet," then you are guilty of creating distinctions among yourselves and of making judgments based on evil motives.

Listen, my dear friends! God chose the poor people of this world to be rich in faith and to possess the kingdom which he promised to those who love him. But you dishonor the poor! Who are the ones who oppress you and drag you before the judges? The rich! They are the ones who speak evil of that good name which has been given to you.

You will be doing the right thing if you obey

the law of the Kingdom, which is found in the scripture, "Love your neighbor as you love yourself." But if you treat people according to their outward appearance, you are guilty of sin, and the Law condemns you as a lawbreaker. Whoever breaks one commandment is guilty of breaking them all. For the same one who said, "Do not commit adultery," also said, "Do not commit murder." Even if you do not commit adultery, you have become a lawbreaker if you commit murder. Speak and act as people who will be judged by the law that sets us free. For God will not show mercy when he judges the person who has not been merciful; but mercy triumphs over judgment.

James 2.1-13

Love does good and does not seek revenge

To conclude: you must all have the same attitude and the same feelings; love one another, and be kind and humble with one another. Do not pay back evil with evil or cursing with cursing; instead, pay back with a blessing, because a blessing is what God promised to give you when he called you. As the scripture says,

"If you want to enjoy life
and wish to see good times,
you must keep from speaking evil
and stop telling lies.
You must turn away from evil and do good;
you must strive for peace with all your
heart.

> For the Lord watches over the righteous
> and listens to their prayers;
> but he opposes those who do evil."

Who will harm you if you are eager to do what is good? But even if you should suffer for doing what is right, how happy you are! Do not be afraid of anyone, and do not worry. But have reverence for Christ in your hearts, and honor him as Lord. Be ready at all times to answer anyone who asks you to explain the hope you have in you, but do it with gentleness and respect. Keep your conscience clear, so that when you are insulted, those who speak evil of your good conduct as followers of Christ will become ashamed of what they say. For it is better to suffer for doing good, if this should be God's will, than for doing evil.

1 Peter 3.8-17

We love because God first loved us

Dear friends, let us love one another, because love comes from God. Whoever loves is a child of God and knows God. Whoever does not love does not know God, for God is love. And God showed his love for us by sending his only Son into the world, so that we might have life through him. This is what love is: it is not that we have loved God, but that he loved us and sent his Son to be the means by which our sins are forgiven.

Dear friends, if this is how God loved us, then we should love one another. No one has ever seen God, but if we love one another, God lives in union with us, and his love is made perfect in us.

We are sure that we live in union with God and that he lives in union with us, because he has given us his Spirit. And we have seen and tell others that the Father sent his Son to be the Savior of the world. If we declare that Jesus is the Son of God, we live in union with God and God lives in union with us. And we ourselves know and believe the love which God has for us.

God is love, and those who live in love live in union with God and God lives in union with them. Love is made perfect in us in order that we may have courage on the Judgment Day; and we will have it because our life in this world is the same as Christ's. There is no fear in love; perfect love drives out all fear. So then, love has not been made perfect in anyone who is afraid, because fear has to do with punishment.

We love because God first loved us. If we say we love God, but hate others, we are liars. For we cannot love God, whom we have not seen, if we do not love others, whom we have seen. The command that Christ has given us is this: whoever loves God must love others also.

1 John 4.7-21

Review and reflect

1. In the first section of this chapter, what do you think James means when he says, "If you treat people according to their outward appearance, you are guilty of sin, and the Law condemns you as a lawbreaker"? Can you think of times in your life when you've seen people treated unfairly based on their outward appearance? Have you ever based opinions about others on their outward appearance? If so, why do you think you did that? Did you change your opinion later? If so, what made you change?

2. Have you ever been judged by your outward appearance or blamed for something you didn't do? How did that make you feel?

3. In the section "Love does good and does not seek revenge," Peter talks about love "in action." Highlight and list all the phrases that illustrate what love enables you to do or not do. Compare this list with the one you prepared earlier for question #2 in the section, **Ask Paul about God's Love.** *How are these lists different? How are they the same?*

4. In the section "We love because God first loved us," what do you think John means when he says, "God is love"?

5. What did God do to show love for us?

6. John says that "perfect love drives out all fear." Can you think of a time when your fear kept you from acting in a loving way toward another person? Can you think of a time when your love for someone gave you courage? What were these times like for you? Did you feel that God was close, or far off when you were going through these experiences? Explain.

ASK JESUS ABOUT GOD'S LOVE

Because of love, God gave his son

As Moses lifted up the bronze snake on a pole in the desert, in the same way the Son of Man must be lifted up, so that everyone who believes in him may have eternal life. For God loved the world so much that he gave his only Son, so that everyone who believes in him may not die but have eternal life. For God did not send his Son into the world to be its judge, but to be its savior.

John 3.14-17

Because of love, Jesus was willing to die for us

"I am the good shepherd, who is willing to die for the sheep. When the hired man, who is not a shepherd and does not own the sheep, sees a wolf coming, he leaves the sheep and runs away; so the wolf snatches the sheep and scatters them. The hired man runs away because he is only a hired man and does not care about the sheep. I am the good shepherd. As the Father knows me and I know the Father, in the same way I know my sheep and they know me. And I am willing to die for them. There are other sheep which belong to me that are not in this sheep pen. I must bring them, too; they will listen to my voice, and they will become one flock with one shepherd.

"The Father loves me because I am willing to give up my life, in order that I may receive it back again. No one takes my life away from me. I give it up of my own free will. I have the right to give it up, and I have the right to take it back. This is what my Father has commanded me to do."

John 10.11-18

Because of love, Jesus prayed for his followers

"I pray for them. I do not pray for the world but for those you gave me, for they belong to you. All I have is yours, and all you have is mine; and my glory is shown through them. And now I am coming to you; I am no longer in the world, but they are in the world. Holy Father! Keep them safe by the power of your name, the name you gave me, so that they may be one just as you and I are one. While I was with them, I kept them safe by the power of your name, the name you gave me. I protected them, and not one of them was lost, except the man who was bound to be lost— so that the scripture might come true. And now I am coming to you, and I say these things in the world so that they might have my joy in their hearts in all its fullness. I gave them your message, and the world hated them, because they do not belong to the world, just as I do not belong to the world. I do not ask you to take them out of the world, but I do ask you to keep them safe from the Evil One. Just as I do not belong to the world, they do not belong to the world. Dedicate them to yourself by means of the truth; your word is truth. I sent them into the world, just as you sent me into the world. And for their sake I dedicate myself to you, in order that they, too, may be truly dedicated to you.

"I pray not only for them, but also for those who believe in me because of their message. I pray that they may all be one. Father! May they be in us, just as you are in me and I am in you. May they be one, so that the world will believe that you sent me. I gave them the same glory you gave me, so that they may be one, just as you and I are one: I in them and you in me, so that they may be completely one, in order that the world may know that you sent me and that you love them as you love me."

John 17.9-23

The Holy Spirit and peace come to those who love Jesus

"If you love me, you will obey my commandments. I will ask the Father, and he will give you another Helper, who will stay with you forever. He is the Spirit, who reveals the truth about God. The world cannot receive him, because it cannot see him or know him. But you know him, because he remains with you and is in you.

"When I go, you will not be left alone; I will

come back to you. In a little while the world will see me no more, but you will see me; and because I live, you also will live. When that day comes, you will know that I am in my Father and that you are in me, just as I am in you.

"Those who accept my commandments and obey them are the ones who love me. My Father will love those who love me; I too will love them and reveal myself to them."

Judas (not Judas Iscariot) said, "Lord, how can it be that you will reveal yourself to us and not to the world?"

Jesus answered him, "Those who love me will obey my teaching. My Father will love them, and my Father and I will come to them and live with them. Those who do not love me do not obey my teaching. And the teaching you have heard is not mine, but comes from the Father, who sent me.

"I have told you this while I am still with you. The Helper, the Holy Spirit, whom the Father will send in my name, will teach you everything and make you remember all that I have told you.

"Peace is what I leave with you; it is my own peace that I give you. I do not give it as the world does. Do not be worried and upset; do not be afraid. You heard me say to you, 'I am leaving, but I will come back to you.' If you loved me, you would be glad that I am going to the Father; for he is greater than I. I have told you this now before it all happens, so that when it does happen, you will believe. I cannot talk with you much longer, because the ruler of this world is coming. He has no power over me, but the world must know that I love the Father; that is why I do everything as he commands me.

"Come, let us go from this place."

John 14.15-31

Love makes us willing to die for others

"I am the vine, and you are the branches. Those who remain in me, and I in them, will bear much fruit; for you can do nothing without me. Those who do not remain in me are thrown out like a branch and dry up; such branches are gathered up and thrown into the fire, where they are burned. If you remain in me and my words remain in you, then you will ask for anything you wish, and you shall have it. My Father's glory is shown by your bearing much fruit; and in this way you become my disciples. I love you just as the Father loves me; remain in my love. If you obey my commands, you will remain in my love, just as I have obeyed my Father's commands and remain in his love.

"I have told you this so that my joy may be in you and that your joy may be complete. My commandment is this: love one another, just as I love you. The greatest love you can have for your friends is to give your life for them. And you are my friends if you do what I command you. I do not call you servants any longer, because servants do not know what their master is doing. Instead,

I call you friends, because I have told you everything I heard from my Father. You did not choose me; I chose you and appointed you to go and bear much fruit, the kind of fruit that endures. And so the Father will give you whatever you ask of him in my name. This, then, is what I command you: love one another."

John 15.5-17

Review and reflect

1. What promise from God is given in the section "Because of love, God gave his son"? When you think of a judge, what characteristics come to mind? What characteristics come to mind when you hear the word "savior"? Which of these characteristics seem to fit Jesus? Which ones don't?

2. Jesus says that he is the "good shepherd." As a good shepherd, what is Jesus willing to do? Underline or highlight these words. What does Jesus say about the "hired man"? Underline or highlight these words (use a different color if possible). Compare the good shepherd with the hired hand. Who showed greater concern for the sheep? Do you love anyone or anything in this way? Explain.

3. In the section "Because of love, Jesus prayed for his followers," Jesus offered a prayer shortly before he was to die. Circle the word "pray" and notice how many times it appears in the pas-

sage. List the things Jesus prayed for. In the last paragraph Jesus prayed for people who hadn't even been born yet. What did he especially want these people to have? Why? Do you ever argue or fight with others? What do you think onlookers would think about your faith in Jesus if they saw you arguing?

4. Have you ever had to say good-bye to someone you thought you might never see again? How did you feel? What did you do?

5. In the section "The Holy Spirit and peace come to those who love Jesus," where did Jesus tell his disciples he was going? What did he say he would do for the disciples after he left them? What does this tell you about Jesus' love for his disciples?

6. In what ways do you think the Holy Spirit helps people today? In what ways does the Holy Spirit help you?

7. What do you think the difference is between the peace Jesus gives to his followers and the peace the world gives?

8. What does Jesus promise to those who love him?

9. In the last section of this chapter, Jesus says, "I am the vine, and you are the branches." What two kinds of branches are described in this pas-

sage? What do you think it means for a Christian to be "a branch" in the world today? Do you think it would be hard sometimes to "remain in" Jesus? Describe the time that it would be hardest. What can you do to "remain in" Jesus' love during such times?

10. Find and highlight Jesus' commandment in the last paragraph of the last section of this chapter. Copy it on an index card and try to memorize it. In obeying this commandment, how should you act toward others? Compare your response with those you prepared for question #3 in the chapter, **Ask Moses about God's Love,** and question #1 in the chapter, **Ask Paul about God's Love.**